The Story of Football

Written by Grant Bage

Contents

Introduction	2
Growth of the game	4
Players	14
Equipment	24
Cups and competitions	30
Fans then and now	36
The business of football	42
Conclusion	46
Glossary	52
Index	53
Football timeline	54

Collins

Introduction

All over the world, boys, girls, women and men play football and support football teams. Football is taught in schools and played for fun in streets, parks and open spaces.

Yet football is more than just fun. Each week in every continent, millions of people buy expensive tickets to go to games played in vast stadiums by highly-paid players.

a fan's view at Barcelona's stadium

Every day, millions of people in hundreds of different countries watch football on TVs and computers, listen to football on radios and read about football in newspapers and magazines.

But the modern sport of football was only invented about 150 years ago. Why did football grow? How did a game that started with brutal battles over a ball, in school yards and on village greens, become one of the world's richest and most popular sports?

This book answers these questions by piecing together facts and true stories. Each piece of the jigsaw has its own tale to tell: football's rules, players, kit, cups, clubs and fans all have histories behind them. Read on to discover the full story.

Growth of the game

Roots

Nobody will ever know for certain when a round ball was first kicked by a human foot, but we do know that people have always played games.

The ancient Greeks enjoyed many sports. Designs on pots and speeches from Greek plays describe people throwing and kicking balls. This description was written by an ancient Greek called Antiphanes around 400 BCE: "Pass out. Throw a long one … down, up, a short one. Pass it back. Get back!"

an ancient Greek ball game

Around 1st century, in ancient China, something called "kick-ball" was played.

The poet Li Yu wrote "A round ball and a square goal … the ball is like the full moon, and the two teams stand opposed."

This pot lid from ancient China shows boys kicking a ball.

When Europeans first sailed west to Central America over 500 years ago, they brought back many things: tomatoes, potatoes, chocolate, silver and gold. They also saw, for the first time, round balls made of rubber. These were used in games that Native Americans had been playing for hundreds of years. To Europeans, a solid ball that bounced was something special!

Although such ancient games were skilful and interesting, it was from different roots that modern football would grow.

This figure of a ball-player comes from Central America, around 100–400 CE.

Over 700 years ago, a game called "football" was played in England. We know this because King Edward II of England passed a law in 1314 to stop football in London's streets. Players of football could even be sent to prison. Why? Because crowds chasing a ball down narrow alleys in medieval towns caused injury, damage and sometimes death.

This early version of football seemed to have few clear rules. Teams could number hundreds of people. Yet more than 500 years after the king of England first tried to ban it, large crowds in towns and villages across 19th-century Britain still gathered to fight over a ball.

These events were called football, but they looked nothing like modern football. Games happened perhaps once a year. They were a mixture of festival and fighting; one half of a town or village battled against the other half. Goals were scored by getting a ball across a river, or to a certain street. There was a lot of kicking, but mostly of other people and not the ball! Some of these games still take place.

the Ashbourne Shrovetide football match in Ashbourne, Derbyshire

Rules

Games without rules turn into big arguments: anyone who has been in a school playground knows that!

The clearest rule in modern football, also sometimes called "soccer", is that "only goalkeepers can pick up the ball". This rule makes it very different from modern rugby – a game in which any player can catch, throw or kick the ball.

The different rules of soccer and rugby were first written down around 150 years ago. Students at the University of Cambridge quarrelled for eight hours, before writing down just 11 rules for football in 1856. Rule seven was "a goal is when the ball is kicked through the flag posts and under the string". But players could still catch the ball. A football club in Sheffield printed similar rules in the 1850s.

By 1867, a group of friends in London had started the Football Association (FA). They said soccer players could no longer handle the ball. In 1871, a similar group, the Rugby Football Union, went the other way. The modern sports of soccer and rugby were born, and it was soccer that became known as "football".

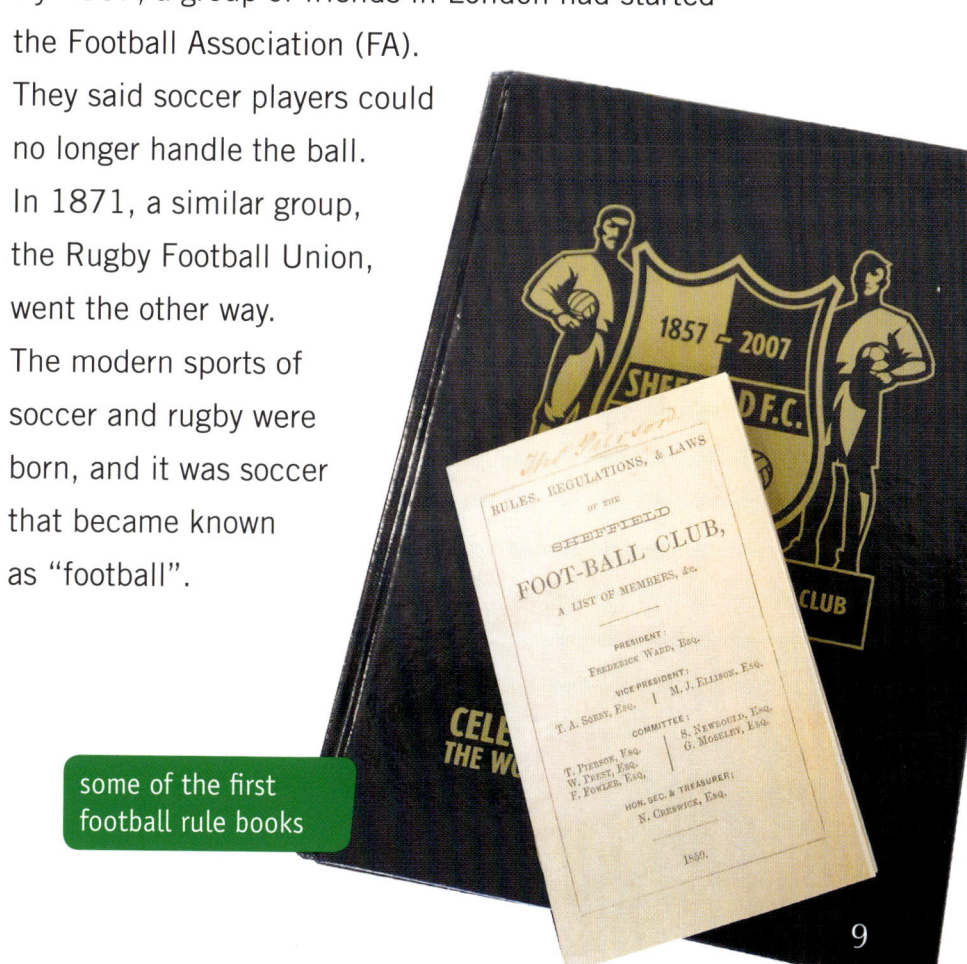

some of the first football rule books

Goals

Now that the Football Association had agreed clear rules, competitions could happen. In 1872, the FA Cup was started in England, and a similar one began in Scotland the year after.

The first three English FA Cup Finals were played with tape stretched between the goalposts. It caused arguments when the ball hit the tape: had it gone under or over? So a solid **crossbar** was introduced, made of wood or metal. By 1882, most football grounds had them.

the 1892 FA Cup Final between West Bromwich Albion and Aston Villa (score 3–0)

Striker Wayne Rooney watches the ball hit the back of the net.

Then, in 1889, another bright idea came along. During an important game, the players quarrelled about whether somebody really had scored. A football fan called John Alexander Brodie, who was watching, wondered how he could stop all that. So he invented the goal net!

In 2013, the English Premier League brought in an electronic system. Cameras and computers could now tell the referee whether a ball had crossed the goal line. But a ball nestling in the back of a net is still the clearest sign of a goal.

Referees

Anybody can enjoy playing football for fun, but when it gets competitive, somebody is needed to enforce the rules.

In soccer's early days, each team chose an **umpire** from their friends. The two umpires then made decisions together. A referee was only needed if

Manchester United win the European Cup in 1968 – but not without an argument.

the umpires disagreed. This didn't work when there were cups to win, so in 1891 referees took over. The umpires became assistants, running round the edge of the pitch holding small flags.

A referee blows his whistle in a game that kicked off in 1907.

This change was very unpopular. In 1897, a referee in Scotland was chased by fans who were cross about decisions made in a game. Six arrests were made: five for throwing eggs at him, and the sixth for pulling his nose. Such bad behaviour happened so often that, in 1908, referees from across England joined together in a Union. Referees did a hard job for fun, not money, and they needed to look after each other.

In modern times, referees at top matches are highly trained and well paid. To make sure players respect them, they keep fit, practise regularly and are watched by other referees to test how good they really are.

This modern referee shows clearly that she is the one in charge.

Players
Fun or money?

People paid to do something are called "**professionals**". If they do it just for fun, they are "**amateurs**". In football's early days, the best players were amateurs. They'd learnt to play at school or university. Most came from richer families, had more time to practise and didn't need to earn money from football. They didn't like professionals, who often had poor backgrounds and less education.

an amateur team from a famous London school called Harrow

In the 1870s, England and Scotland both started FA Cup competitions. Amateur teams won every year. Then in 1883, Blackburn Olympic became the first professional team to win the English Cup, beating former pupils from the rich and famous school of Eton. When the Blackburn team was welcomed home from London by adoring crowds and a brass band, some amateurs grew to dislike the professionals even more.

the Blackburn Olympic team and their captain

The amateurs never won the FA Cup again, but as football grew, bigger crowds meant more money. For example, in 1878, Everton Football Club played their first game on a park in Liverpool. The players did it for fun and put the goalposts up themselves. Ten years later, Everton held their first league game, watched by a crowd of 8,000. Why shouldn't players share in the money that was made?

From rags to riches

Modern professional football makes a few players rich. Fara Williams won league titles in 2013 and 2014 with Liverpool Ladies Football Club. She played for England in front of huge crowds, at World Cups in 2007, 2011 and 2015. Yet Fara was homeless aged 17, and for six years kept her homelessness secret from team-mates. Football gave Fara hope of a better life: "I had that focus and belief I was good at something. That's an incredible thing when it feels like you've got nothing else."

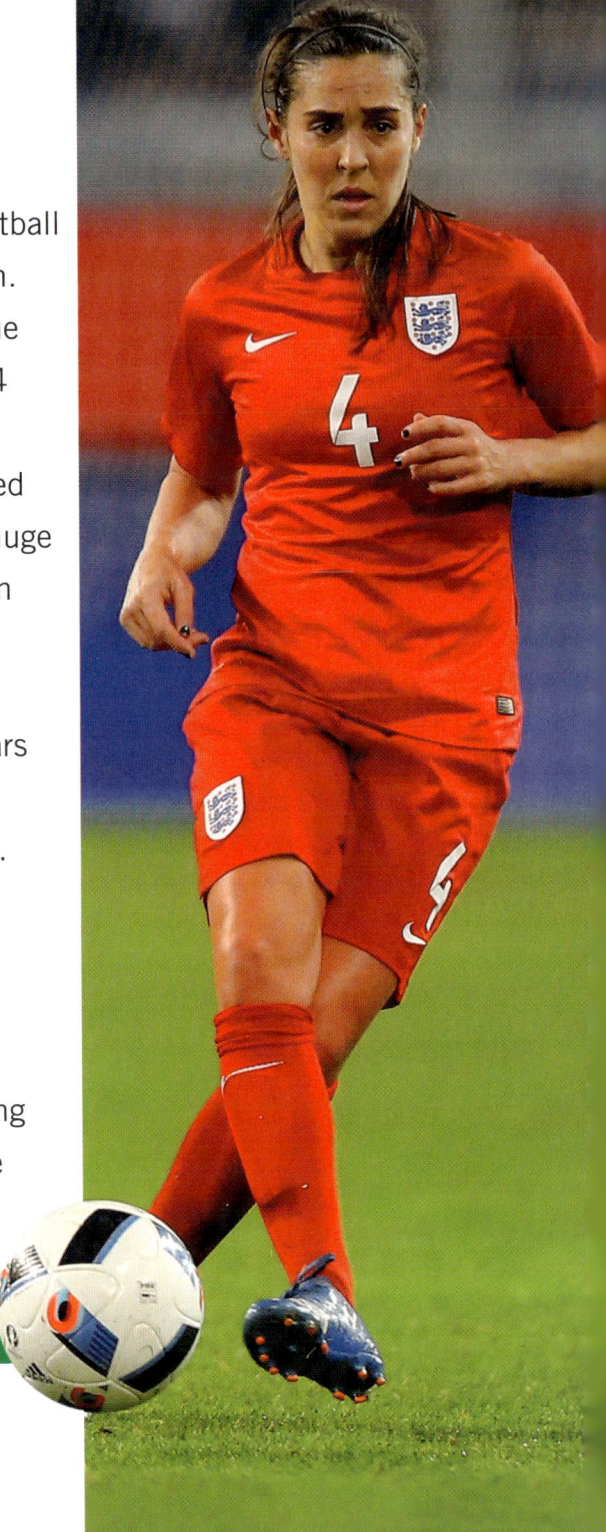

Fara Williams

Professional footballers 100 years ago needed to earn money too, but in 1900, English clubs voted to pay players no more than £4 a week. Most got less, although some clubs paid more in secret to attract the best players. Manchester City paid over £6 a week. They were found out in 1905. As punishment, their best players were sold to other clubs at an **auction**. Manchester United bought three of them!

By 1960, just £20 a week was still the maximum wage. In 1961, professional footballers said they'd stop playing matches unless this changed. The clubs backed down. Top footballers can now earn massive wages!

Billy Meredith was a star player in the 1900s, who played for both Manchester City and Manchester United.

Fitness and health

When the First World War began in 1914, there were thousands of professional players across Europe, and Southern and Central America. These professionals were good footballers, but weren't always fit. For many years, football training wasn't yet a science.

Modern footballers are different. To succeed they must stay fit, eat healthy food and train every day to improve their ball skills. Healthy habits start early so professional football clubs run girls' and boys' teams for young children. If good enough as teenagers, they join academies, mixing football and education. A few of the best academy players then become professionals.

Queen's Park Rangers team in training, 1922

Fabrice Muamba did everything right. He moved to London from Zaire (now called Democratic Republic of the Congo) as an 11-year-old refugee. He couldn't speak English but he worked hard at school and at football. Soon Fabrice was in Arsenal's academy, later being bought by Bolton for five million pounds. But nobody knew this fit young man had a rare illness. In 2012, during a game shown on TV, Fabrice had a heart attack. His heart stopped for 78 minutes. Fabrice can no longer play professional football but is glad just to be alive: "I have much to be thankful for." Football science is still learning lessons and now all young professional footballers' hearts are tested.

Players then and now

Tom Finney and David Beckham were two of the England team's best-ever players. Both became famous, despite living very different lives.

David Beckham

David Beckham was born in London in 1975. He played football for 20 years, first for Manchester United and then from 2003 for clubs in Spain, Italy, the USA and France. Beckham started modelling when still playing football and continued after retiring. He's a multi-millionaire, not just from football but from perfume, TV, advertising and many other businesses. Sales of football shirts and boots linked to Beckham's name have been worth over a thousand million pounds.

Tom Finney

Tom Finney was born in 1922, next door to Preston North End's ground. He only ever played for Preston and England, scoring 247 goals in 556 games. As a child, he was short, skinny and often ill, but so talented that Preston still signed him aged 15. Then the Second World War began and Finney drove tanks for the army. Football started again in 1945, and until 1960, Finney was one of the world's best players. During his whole career, Finney was never booked or sent off. Yet his footballing wage was less than £30 a week. Finney earned more working as a plumber: his nickname was "the Preston Plumber".

Managers then and now

Football clubs also need **managers**. Both these women did that job, about 100 years apart.

Nettie Honeyball

Nettie Honeyball organised one of the first female football teams. In 1894, she put an advert in a London newspaper, seeking women to play football. Around 30 replied. Most had enjoyed watching football but now they wanted to play themselves. A male professional footballer from Tottenham Hotspur was their **coach**. During the next two years, they played in front of large crowds across England and Scotland, raising money for charity. Nettie Honeyball's aim was "to show the world that women are not the 'ornamental and useless' creatures men have pictured".

22

Hope Powell

Hope Powell played football for 20 years, making 66 appearances for England and scoring 35 goals. She then managed England's women's football team for 15 years from 1998, before being sacked in 2013. Powell changed many things. More people trained to coach girls and women, and from 2009 the best female players were paid enough for football to become their job. In that year, England's women reached the final of the European championships, and in 2011, the World Cup quarter finals. For over 20 years, they've done better than England's men's team.

Equipment
The ball

Football needs managers, captains and players, but without a ball, nothing can happen.

The earliest footballs were **bladders** from dead animals, blown up like balloons. Then people discovered these balls lasted longer with a leather cover, sewn around the outside. A small ball like this, dating from around 1540, has been discovered in Stirling Castle, Scotland.

This football, found at Stirling Castle, could be the oldest in Europe.

Most animal bladders weren't round or regular in shape, so an English shoemaker called Richard Lindon worked out a better way of making a round ball. In the 1860s, he started using thin balloons of rubber for the inside of footballs. The outside was still leather: 18 pieces sewn together and a narrow opening, through which the rubber "bladder" was stuffed and then laced up like a shoe. He even invented a pump to blow them up.

Leather balls were heavy, and got heavier when it rained, so footballs today are covered in waterproof material. The inside is also more complicated than a simple rubber balloon. They have thin layers of different materials designed to make the ball softer but stronger. Since 1970, every World Cup has had a different design of ball.

South Korea/Japan
2002

Germany
2006

Brazil
2014

South Africa
2010

25

The pitch

When modern football started, pitches had no lines. Instead, four flags were placed where the umpires guessed the pitch corners to be. As football became popular, ways were found to draw lines on grass using chalk or weedkiller. But the first professional football pitches could still be so muddy, and with such rough or bumpy grass, that it was sometimes difficult to play, let alone see the lines.

Modern pitches at professional games are very different. The grass is laid, cut, fed, drained and looked after by teams of people.

> This pitch is being watered before a game, to make the surface smooth and help the ball run fast.

Some pitches have underfloor heating so games can be played even when it's frosty.

Technology has helped develop artificial pitches. These look like grass but are made of plastics and rubber. Because these surfaces can be played on in any weather, and don't need watering, cutting or feeding, they are popular in schools and sports centres. The Women's World Cup in 2015 was the first to be played on such pitches.

Football kit

Muddy pitches, long grass and heavy leather balls meant the first football boots had to be sturdy and tough. Amateurs probably wore work shoes, but it wasn't long before boots were specially designed and sold, just for playing football. In 1891, studs were allowed on the soles, to grip on slippery surfaces.

100 years later, Craig Johnston changed football boots forever. Johnston was born in South Africa, moved to Australia and nearly lost his leg to a bone infection aged six years old, but he went on to play 271 games for Liverpool and win many medals. In the early 1990s, Johnston designed the Predator. This new boot had rubber strips sewn into the leather surface, giving more power when shooting and finer control of the ball.

a Predator football boot from the 1990s

Bristol Academy Women, 2014

the North Team (Ladies), 1895

Football shirts used to be made of rough, thick cotton. Choosing kit was especially difficult for early female players because women then rarely dared to wear shorts or trousers. Remember, women aged under 30 couldn't even vote in Great Britain until 1928!

But football kit gradually became lighter and cheaper to buy, both for women's and men's teams.

Barcelona 2013

Arsenal 1936

Cups and competitions

Leagues and cups

In football's early days, most games were either "friendlies" played for fun, or serious games in "cups". 15,000 people watched Aston Villa win the FA Cup in 1887, and half of them had travelled by train to London from Birmingham. A year later, a man called William McGregor from Aston Villa wrote a letter that would change the world of football.

He realised that football's thousands of fans wanted more games to watch. Something different was needed: a league. So McGregor wrote to 12 professional clubs, from the North or Midlands, inviting them to play each other at home and away. They agreed, and the world's first football league started in England in 1888. By 1892, it had 28 teams in two divisions. Arsenal was the first London club to join in 1893.

Sheffield United playing Tottenham Hotspur in the 1901 FA Cup Final

A rival Southern League started in 1894. Tottenham, a club from that league, won the FA Cup in 1901, but soon the big southern clubs wanted to join the Football League.

By 1920, England had one league with four different divisions. Then, during the next 20 years, professional football leagues spread in countries across Europe and South America.

League football in Germany in the 1930s

Local to global

Today, the best clubs in the football leagues of England, Scotland, Spain, Germany, Italy, Brazil and Argentina aren't just popular in their own countries; they've become world famous.

Clubs from different leagues in Europe or South America also play each other, to become champions of a whole continent.

Real Madrid and the European Cup in 1956

But in the early days, football spread almost by accident. Victoria was queen of the British empire and British people sailed to ports around the world. Many lived and worked in different countries for most of their lives. They played football wherever they went, and started clubs. The idea soon caught on.

Teams started to travel abroad, just to play football. The world's first international match was between Scotland and England, in 1872. The players went by train to the match at Hamilton Crescent in Partick, Scotland.

Chelsea and Tottenham teams sailed to Argentina to play football in the early 1900s, and teams from many different countries visited Britain. One from Basuto in South Africa in 1899 was an early example. In 1920, women footballers from France and England played a series of seven games in both countries, watched by crowds of up to 25,000. Football had become an international sport!

33

The World Cup

Although soccer spread quickly worldwide, it was 1930 before a "World Cup" happened. Amateurs had played football at the Olympic Games since 1912. Why shouldn't the world's best professional footballers also play each other? The first World Cup took place in Uruguay in 1930. The event drew 13 teams and huge crowds. 20,000 Argentinian fans sailed to watch their team lose the final to Uruguay.

a poster for the 1930 World Cup

Teams from Britain didn't enter the World Cup until 1950, and only England went to that year's final in Brazil. Because modern professional football had begun there, English fans and players thought English footballers were the best in the world. That wasn't true. England were beaten by the USA, and then by Spain.

England's finest footballers watched in amazement at the skills being shown, even during beach football in Brazil. England's captain Billy Wright described how children would "bite a little hole in an orange, suck the juice out and the orange then became a ball", with one boy "keeping it up in the air 76 times without touching the ground, great skill."

Women footballers had been playing international matches since the 1920s.

Yet it was not until 1988 that women's football had a World Cup.

France play Belgium: international women's football from the 1930s

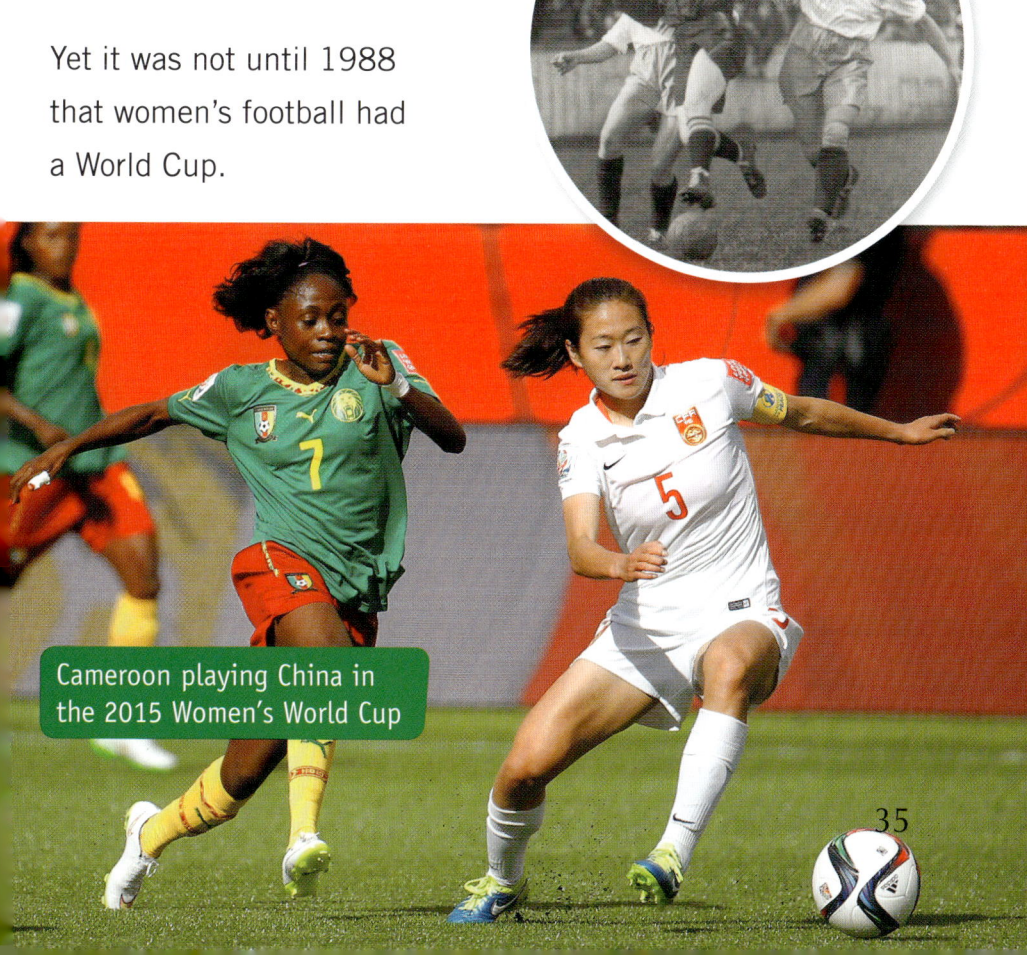

Cameroon playing China in the 2015 Women's World Cup

Fans then and now

Stadiums and terraces

Football became popular with players because it's simple to play and to practise.

Why did football become popular with crowds?

Professional football started in the factory towns of Scotland and Northern England in the 1880s. After working 60 hours a week, people wanted entertainment on Saturday afternoons. It cost sixpence in old money (just 2.5 modern pence) to watch a football match. Some clubs let women in for free: at Preston in April 1885 over 2,000 women turned up! Free places for women were soon stopped because clubs said they were losing too much money.

crowds attend a British Army v Royal Navy football match, February 1910

Clubs wanted the best players, the best players wanted good wages and clubs with bigger grounds made more money. Stamford Bridge Stadium in London opened in 1877, for **athletics**. To fill that stadium, in 1905 a new football club was started: Chelsea. Enormous **terraces** were built and in 1935, 83,000 people stood on them to watch Chelsea play Arsenal.

huge crowds for Chelsea v Arsenal in 1935

Vast terraces could make football grounds difficult places for children. At a big FA Cup game at Leicester in 1925, a schoolboy recalled: "We got in a bit late but I remember being passed down over the heads of the crowd ... to sit next to the pitch, almost touching the grass."

the modern Stamford Bridge – Chelsea's home ground

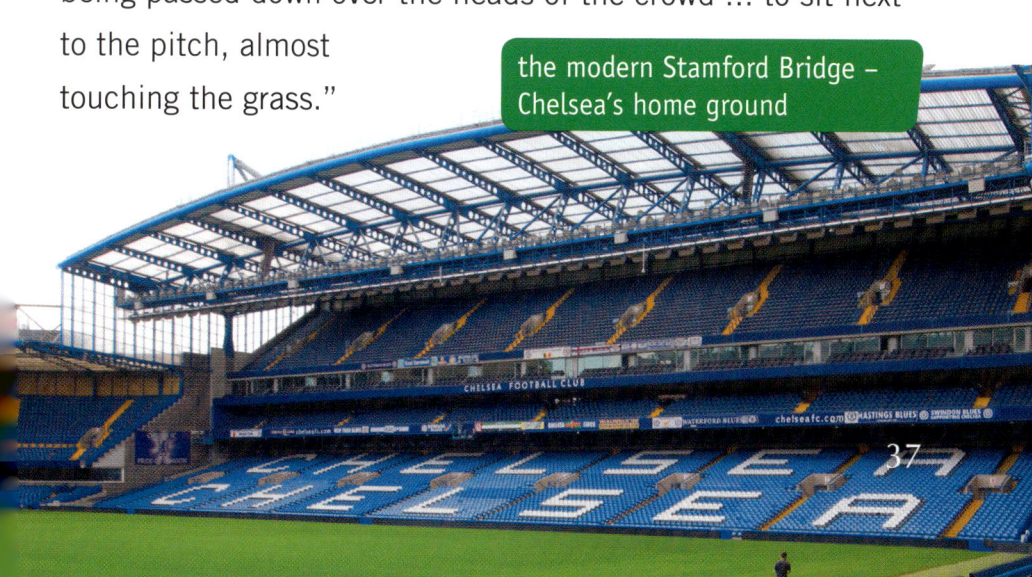

Getting to the match

It takes a lot of time and money to build a football stadium. Brazil's Maracanã Stadium held 200,000 people for the 1950 World Cup Final, most of them standing. Yet building work was not fully finished until 1965!

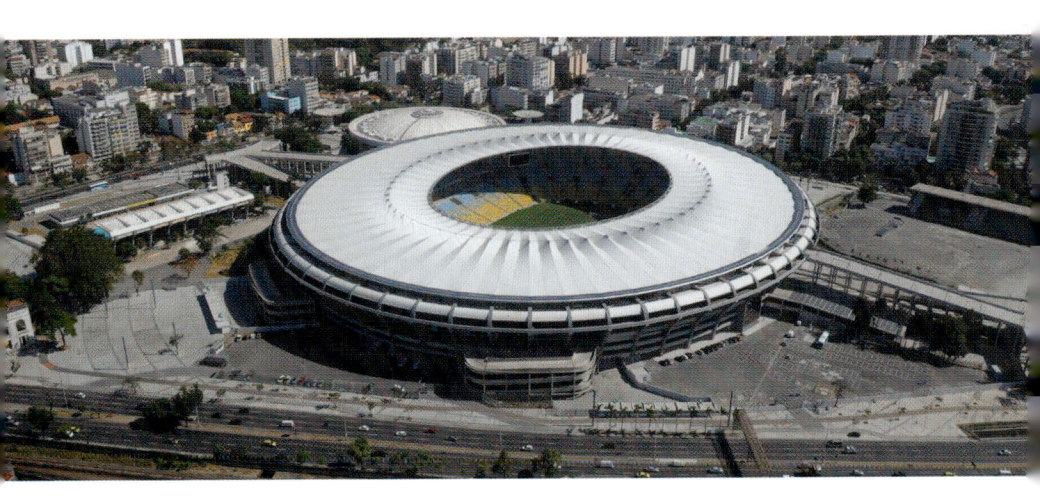

Terraces were important, but players and supporters also needed to reach the ground before a game. Another reason football grew quickly in England and Scotland was that railways joined so many British towns and cities.

Arsenal football club started in South London, but moved to North London in 1913 partly to be closer to bigger railway stations, and draw larger crowds. In 1932, the club even persuaded London's Underground railway company to rename the local tube station "Arsenal".

Using trains at first, and later buses and cars, supporters travelled to games at home and away. For big matches, groups of friends travelled together, making it feel like a holiday.

Football under **floodlights** was first tried in 1878, but not until 1956 were English league games played in the evening. Crowds liked floodlit matches. Floodlights meant people could watch football on weekday evenings as well as Saturday afternoons, and the electric lights made colours crisper and everything look spectacular.

Fans and fun

There are many sensible reasons why people like football, but perhaps some reasons are also mysterious. People watch a few games for fun and then find themselves hooked. They turn into fans. "Fan" is short for "fanatic", a word meaning somebody who believes in something so much that nothing can change it. Some football fans feel that for their team. They love them!

Fans' support is shown in many ways: wearing their team's shirt or buying mugs, pens, slippers, pyjamas, wallpaper, lunchboxes and lots of other things with their club's badge on. Some fans name their children after favourite players, while others haven't missed a match for 30 years. A few fans even ask that after dying, their ashes be scattered on the team's home pitch.

Fans, and not just players, make football entertaining. Their flags, banners, scarves and team shirts are a colourful sight. Fans bring matches to life with their claps, chants and songs. When a goal is scored, fans jump, shout and cheer. Professionals play football for money, for cups and for glory, but the best players also give everything, for the fans.

The business of football

Whose game is it?

Money from millions of fans has turned football into big business, but some of the world's biggest clubs grew from businesses in the first place.

Newton Heath is one example. It was started in 1878 by workers in the carriage department of the Lancashire and Yorkshire railway company. Wearing green and yellow, they played football against other railway companies. The club did well. It attracted fans and paid players, but by 1902 the owners had run out of money. Some rich local people paid the club's debts, bought the club and changed its colours to red and white. They also changed its name: Manchester United was born.

Newton Heath football club in 1890 – before they became Manchester United

fans of FC United of Manchester in 2014

But 103 years later in 2005, Manchester United was sold to new owners. Some fans disagreed and started a new club of their own: FC United of Manchester. By 2015, this new club had built their own ground for nearly 5,000 people. That's a lot smaller than Manchester United's ground which holds 75,000, but the new club is owned by its fans. It can't be sold or taken over, unless the fans agree.

Football and games

Football started as a game but is now a passion, all over the world. For many people, even playing and watching isn't enough. Computer games about being a football player or football manager are bought and played by thousands of children and adults. They spend time and money playing one game that's all about another game!

This isn't new. Table football has been popular since the 1950s. It can be played by two or four people. The "players" are plastic figures about 15 centimetres high, on metal rods. The human's job is to turn and push the rods to get the players in the right place, to "kick" a small ball. There's even a table football World Cup!

Blow football was a cheaper, easier game from around the same time in which children blew air out of tubes the length of a pencil, to steer a light and small plastic ball into some model goals.

Perhaps the most famous football-based game is Subbuteo. Invented in 1947, it's played with tiny figures of footballers (smaller than a child's thumb) standing on round bases.

45

Conclusion
Football past and present

Children across the world love playing and watching football. It'll also make a few of them famous, like the four players in this section.

Alf Ramsey

In 1966, Alf Ramsey managed the England team that won the World Cup at Wembley Stadium. Yet 40 years earlier, Ramsey's childhood home, on the edge of London and over 40 kilometres from Wembley, had no electricity, running water or inside toilet. His walk to school took an hour, and the family was so poor that Ramsey only ever went to one match as a child. The family had no television on which to watch football, or radio to listen to it. Ramsey practised **footwork** with tennis balls, because they were cheaper to buy!

Pele

Pele was born in Brazil, 20 years later than Alf Ramsey. He played against England when Ramsey managed them. Pele's family was also too poor to buy footballs; he practised using a grapefruit or socks stuffed with paper. Aged just 17, Pele scored the only goal of the 1958 World Cup quarter final to knock out Wales, then scored a hat-trick in the semi-final. In the final, he scored two more goals as Brazil beat Sweden. The rest of his career was just as special. During the 1967 Nigerian civil war, the two sides stopped fighting for 48 hours because Pele's club was visiting; everybody wanted to watch the game.

Lionel Messi

Lionel Messi was always smaller than other children. Doctors blamed a hormone deficiency, yet he became one of the world's greatest footballers, winning many cups with Barcelona and captaining his country's team, Argentina. How? Messi's parents were poor, but saved up money for injections to help Lionel grow. Then their cash ran out. Only by moving the family across the world to Barcelona could the injections continue. Messi signed for Barcelona aged 13 years and at 16 made his debut. The rest is history.

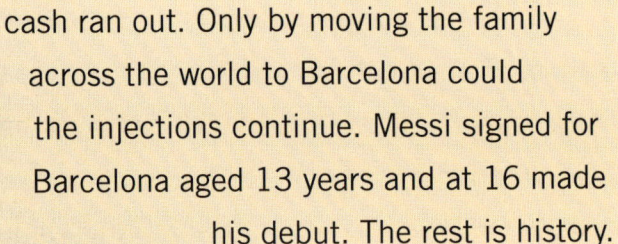

Carli Lloyd

Carli Lloyd's football career reads like fiction, not fact, but every word is true. She started playing football aged five, and as a teenager practised for hours alone. Such determination brought her success. In 2008, Lloyd scored the winning goal in extra time at the women's Olympic football final, against Brazil. In 2012, she scored both Olympic Cup Final goals as the USA beat Japan 2–1. Then it was dream-time in the 2015 Women's World Cup Final. Within the first 16 minutes, she scored three goals. The third was chipped over the goalkeeper's head, from close to the halfway line.

Football forever

For 150 years, football has brought people together from all backgrounds and abilities.

Blind football has been played since 2004, at the Paralympic Games. The ball has a bell inside. Blind footballers judge where the ball is by the sound from that bell.

The Wheelchair Football Association was started in 2005, for people in wheelchairs with electric motors. Athletes with disabilities compete hard, playing to win, but for enjoyment as well.

wheelchair footballers training

Since the 1990s, children as young as 18 months have been joining clubs to learn football: toddlers who are only just walking! But walking football is also a game that was invented in 2011, for people aged 50 and more. In this version of football, players aren't allowed to run, tackle or kick the ball above waist height. Walking football allows older people to enjoy all the fun of the game at a gentler pace.

Football has a long history, but it has changed in the last 20 years too. If it carries on changing, football should have a great future. Who knows: you might even be part of it!

Walking football – Grimsby Ancient Mariners v Hornsea 3G

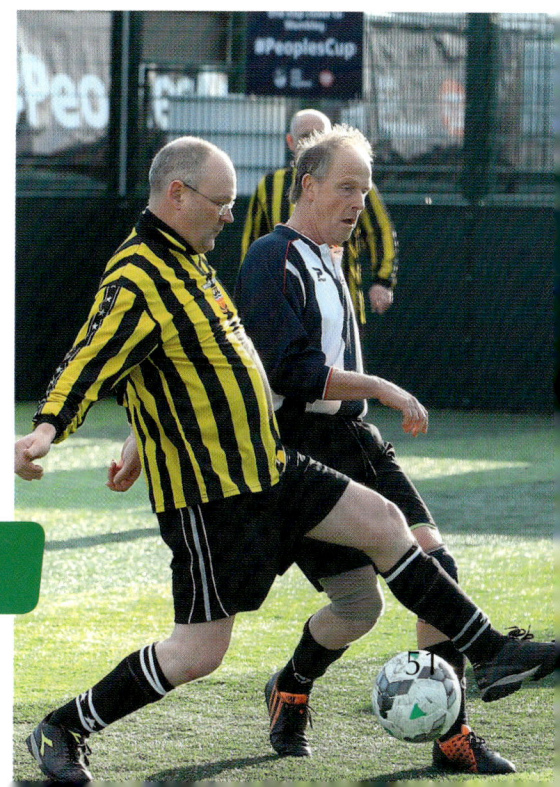

Glossary

athletics   the sport of taking part in running, jumping or throwing competitions

amateurs   people who take part in a sport or activity for the love of it, not for money

auction   a sale in which goods are sold to the person who offers the most money

bladders   bag-like parts of animals' insides, where urine is stored

coach   a person who trains the members of a football team to be better players

crossbar   a horizontal bar between two goalposts

floodlights   high-intensity artificial lights that are used at evening football matches

footwork   skilful use of the feet to manoeuvre the ball

managers   people responsible for running football clubs or teams

professionals   people who take part in a sport or activity as a paid job

terraces   series of concrete steps in a stadium, which spectators stand or sit on

umpire   an official who watches a match and makes sure the rules are kept

Index

amateurs   14–15, 28, 34
ancient China   5
Arsenal   19, 29–30, 37–38
Beckham, David   20
Blackburn Olympic   15
blind football   50
blow football   45
Brazil   25, 32, 34–35, 38, 47, 49
Central America   5, 18
Chelsea   33, 37
Everton   15
FA Cup   10, 15, 30–31, 37
fans   3, 13, 30, 34, 36, 40–43
FC United of Manchester   43
Finney, Tom   20–21
fitness   18
Football Association   9–10, 50
Football League   30–32
Honeyball, Nettie   22
international matches   33, 35
King Edward II   6
kit   3, 28–29
Lloyd, Carli   49

Manchester City   17
Manchester United   12, 17, 20, 42–43
medieval   6
Messi, Lionel   48
Muamba, Fabrice   19
Newton Heath   42
Pele   47
pitches   12, 26–27, 28, 37, 41
Powell, Hope   23
Preston   21, 36
Ramsey, Alf   46–47
rugby   8–9
Subbuteo   45
table football   44
Tottenham   22, 31, 33
training   18, 50
walking football   51
Wheelchair Football Association   50
Williams, Fara   16
Women's World Cup   27, 35, 49
World Cup   16, 23, 25, 27, 34–35, 38, 44, 46–47, 49

53

Football timeline

around 2,400 years ago Ancient Greeks played ball games

around 2,000 years ago "kick-ball" played in Ancient China

1314 law passed to stop "football" being played in London streets

1856 Cambridge University students wrote some rules for football.

1860s Richard Lindon developed a round football.

1867 Football Association (FA) founded

1872 first FA Cup; first international match (Scotland v England)

Early history 1800

14th century a game called "football" played in England

Middle Ages to 19th century rough "football" games played across Britain

1888 Football League began; Blackburn Olympic first professional team to win the FA Cup

1891 referees commonly used in football matches

1894 Nettie Honeyball set up a women's football team.

1920s English football had one league and four divisions.

1930 first World Cup, in Uruguay

1947 football game Subbuteo invented

1950s "table football" and "blow football" popular

1956 English league games began to be played in the evenings as well as weekends.

1900

1961 Professional footballers threatened to strike for more pay.

1966 Alf Ramsey's England team won the World Cup.

1988 first Women's World Cup

2000

2005 Wheelchair Football Association founded

2013 English Premier League brought in goal-line technology to assist referees.

Ideas for reading

Written by Clare Dowdall, PhD
Lecturer and Primary Literacy Consultant

Reading objectives:
- make comparisons within and across books
- explore the meaning of words in context
- make predictions from details stated and implied
- retrieve, record and present information from non-fiction
- explain and discuss their understanding of what they have read, including through formal presentations and debates, maintaining a focus on the topic and using notes where necessary

Spoken language objectives:
- articulate and justify answers, arguments and opinions

Curriculum links: History – British history, PE – competitive games

Resources: ICT, pens and paper

Build a context for reading

- Ask children who play football to suggest why it is such a popular game around the world. Pool knowledge about current football superstars and tournaments.
- Read the blurb together and discuss what makes football a great spectator sport. Check children understand the word and link it to other known words, e.g. spectacle.
- Ask children to suggest how football might have changed over time and why.

Understand and apply reading strategies

- Read pp2-3 together. Ask children to predict how the rules and kit for football may have changed over the years.
- Ask children to read pp4-7 silently. When they have finished, ask them to retrieve and share key facts about the roots of the game. Support them to recount accurately, making reference to the text.